This groovy messenger bag offers an updated nod to the leather-link bags of the 70s. Pick two kraft-tex colors and get your groove on!

The links on the bag and wristlet, as well as the strap accent on the wristlet and key fob, are made using kraft-tex—C&T Publishing's washable paper fabric that looks and behaves like leather. All you need are regular sewing supplies to work with this innovative product.

I used a heavyweight cotton denim for the body of the bag, but you could certainly use lighter fabrics—such as home dec–weight prints or even cotton quilting fabrics—provided you interface them adequately to keep their shape.

For those using a computerized embroidery machine, a stitching file is available to download. For digital cutters, an SVG file (a special file for that cutter) is also available to download. For those without these computerized devices, patterns for the link shapes are included in this booklet, so you can cut them yourself.

MATERIALS

The materials below make one bag, wristlet, and key fob.
Adjust amounts if you're using fabrics of varying widths.

kraft-tex Designer Roll Prewashed & Hand-Dyed (by C&T Publishing):
1 roll (18½" × 28½") each of Turquoise (Color 1) and Greenery (Color 2) for links, inside pocket detail, wristlet strap, and key fob

Main fabric: 1 yard of 58"–60"-wide white cotton denim for bag body, wristlet, and key fob

Lining fabric: 1 yard of 40"-wide coordinating quilting-weight cotton print for bag and wristlet

Interfacing:
1 yard of 20"-wide heavyweight fusible interfacing for body of bag (I used Pellon 808 Craft Fuse.)

Optional: 1⅓ yards of 20"-wide lightweight fusible interfacing for lining and wristlet (I used Pellon 911FF Fusible Featherweight.) *Omit if you are satisfied with the weight of your lining fabric.*

HARDWARE AND NOTIONS

White machine embroidery thread

Bag hardware:
2 rectangle rings 1½" wide
1 slide buckle 1½" wide

Key fob hardware: 1 set of
1¼" clamp base with split key ring

Zipper: 9" for wristlet (It will be trimmed to size.)

TOOLS

Sharp scissors

Craft knife

Rotary cutter and mat

Clear ruler

Disappearing-ink fabric marker

Card stock or quilting template plastic (if cutting links by hand)

tips

- I found that by having my 4½″ × 4½″ squares of kraft-tex and tear-away stabilizer cut, stacked, and ready to go, I could embroider a couple squares here and there until I had enough. Then I kept the embroidered links by my favorite chair and trimmed them as I had time. Before I knew it, my links were ready to stitch and the bag itself came together quickly.

- If you have embroidery editing software and hoops larger than 4″ × 4″, you can "merge" the files in the software to be able to stitch more links per hooping.

- Etsy.com is a great resource for purse and key fob hardware.

CUTTING

Main fabric

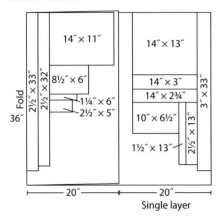

Messenger Bag

- Cut 1 piece 14″ × 11″ for front.
- Cut 1 piece 14″ × 11″ for back.
- Cut 1 piece 14″ × 13″ for flap.
- Cut 1 piece 3″ × 33″ for gusset.
- Cut 1 piece 14″ × 3″ for upper link cover band.
- Cut 1 piece 14″ × 2¾″ for lower link cover band.
- Cut 2 pieces 2½″ × 33″ for strap top side.
- Cut 2 pieces 2½″ × 32″ for strap bottom side.
- Cut 2 pieces 2½″ × 5″ for hardware tabs.
- Cut 1 piece 10″ × 6½″ for inner pocket.

Wristlet

- Cut 1 piece 8½″ × 6″ for front.
- Cut 1 piece 8½″ × 6″ for back.
- Cut 2 pieces 1¼″ × 6″ for side link cover bands.
- Cut 1 piece 1½″ × 13″ for strap.

Key Fob

- Cut 1 piece 2½″ × 13″ for strap.

Lining fabric

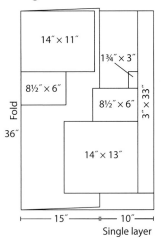

14″ × 11″

1¾″ × 3″

8½″ × 6″

8½″ × 6″

3″ × 33″

14″ × 13″

Fold

36″

|— 15″ —|—— 10″ ——|

Single layer

Heavyweight fusible interfacing

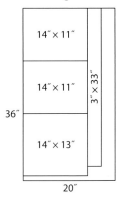

14″ × 11″

14″ × 11″

3″ × 33″

36″

14″ × 13″

20″

Messenger Bag

- Cut 1 piece 14″ × 11″ for front.
- Cut 1 piece 14″ × 11″ for back.
- Cut 1 piece 14″ × 13″ for flap.
- Cut 1 piece 3″ × 33″ for gusset.

Messenger Bag

- Cut 1 piece 14″ × 11″ for front.
- Cut 1 piece 14″ × 11″ for back.
- Cut 1 piece 14″ × 13″ for flap.
- Cut 1 piece 3″ × 33″ for gusset.

Wristlet

- Cut 1 piece 8½″ × 6″ for front.
- Cut 1 piece 8½″ × 6″ for back.
- Cut 1 piece 8½″ × 6″ for front contrast panel, under links.
- Cut 1 piece 1¼″ × 3″ for zipper tabs.

Lightweight fusible interfacing

Optional. Omit if you are satisfied with the weight of your lining fabric.

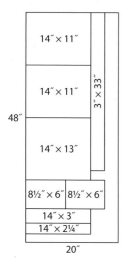

Messenger Bag

- Cut 1 piece 14″ × 11″ for front lining piece.
- Cut 1 piece 14″ × 11″ for back lining piece.
- Cut 1 piece 14″ × 13″ for flap lining piece.
- Cut 1 piece 3″ × 33″ for gusset lining piece.

kraft-tex

Color 1 (Turquoise)

- If using a computerized embroidery machine, cut 11 squares 4½″ × 4½″ to embroider/cut links (10 squares for Messenger Bag, 1 square for Wristlet).

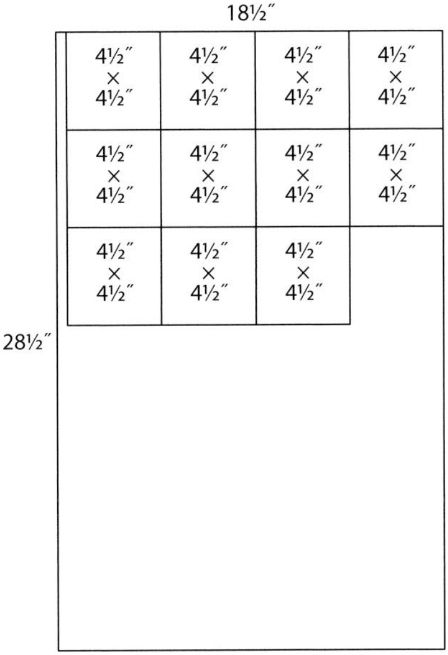

18½″

4½″ × 4½″	4½″ × 4½″	4½″ × 4½″	4½″ × 4½″
4½″ × 4½″	4½″ × 4½″	4½″ × 4½″	4½″ × 4½″
4½″ × 4½″	4½″ × 4½″	4½″ × 4½″	

28½″

Color 2 (Greenery)

- Cut 1 piece 13″ × 1″ for Key Fob strap.
- Cut 1 piece 13″ × ½″ for Wristlet strap.
- Cut 1 piece 8½″ × ¾″ for inner pocket detail.
- If using a computerized embroidery machine, cut 9 squares 4½″ × 4½″ to embroider/cut links (7 squares for Messenger Bag, 2 squares for Wristlet).

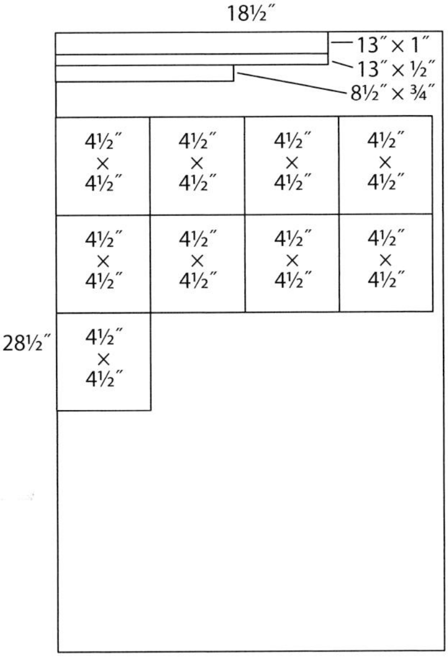

18½″

—13″ × 1″
—13″ × ½″
—8½″ × ¾″

4½″ × 4½″	4½″ × 4½″	4½″ × 4½″	4½″ × 4½″
4½″ × 4½″	4½″ × 4½″	4½″ × 4½″	4½″ × 4½″
4½″ × 4½″			

28½″

Creating the Links

Embroidering the Links

NOTE

The links that are cut using a digital cutter or cut by hand (see Cutting the Links, page 13) will not have stitching around the edges.

USING MACHINE EMBROIDERY

MACHINE EMBROIDERY FILES

For machine embroidery, there are two files (**3links** and **2linksandoval**) available at:

tinyurl.com/80089-pattern-download

- **3links** This file stitches 3 links in the 4″ × 4″ hoop. Stitch this file on 10 Turquoise squares and 9 Greenery squares.

- **2linksandoval** This file stitches the oval center link for the wristlet plus 2 links. Stitch this file on 1 Turquoise square.

For the Messenger Bag, you will need:
   28 Turquoise links • 21 Greenery links

For the Wristlet, you will need:
   2 Turquoise links • 1 Turquoise oval • 4 Greenery links

1. Download the embroidery files.

2. Send the **3links** file (see Machine Embroidery Files, previous page) to your machine.

3. Hoop a piece of tear-away stabilizer. Place the hoop in the machine.

4. Center a 4½″ Turquoise kraft-tex square on the hooped stabilizer. Carefully hold the piece in place while the machine takes the first few stitches. Stitch the design.

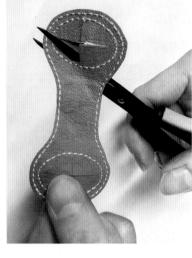

5. Remove the hoop from the machine, and remove the work from the hoop.

6. Carefully tear the stabilizer away from the back of the embroidered kraft-tex piece.

7. Using the sharp scissors, cut around the outside stitching of the links at 1/16″ from the stitching.

8. To cut out the inner ovals of the links, use the craft knife to cut a small slice in the center of each oval. Hold the link in your hand and have the scissors come up through the hole from the bottom of the link.

9. Trim inside the hole 1/16″ from the stitching.

10. Repeat Steps 3–9, using 9 of the remaining Turquoise squares and the 9 Greenery squares.

11. Stitch the **2linksandoval** file (see Machine Embroidery Files, page 10) on the remaining Turquoise square, following Steps 1–9.

Cutting the Links

OPTION 1: USING A DIGITAL CUTTER

SVG FILES

For a digital cutter, there are two SVG files (**link** and **oval**) available at:

tinyurl.com/80089-pattern-download

For the Messenger Bag, you will need:
28 Turquoise links • 21 Greenery links

For the Wristlet, you will need:
2 Turquoise links • 1 Turquoise oval • 4 Greenery links

1. Download the SVG files.

2. kraft-tex comes in 18½"-wide rolls. Use this measurement to determine placement of the link design. Follow the manufacturer's instructions for sending the design to your cutter.

3. The link should measure 3⅜" × 1½". It may have to be adjusted in the cutter software.

4. Cut 30 Turquoise links, 1 Turquoise oval, and 25 Greenery links.

OPTION 2: CUTTING BY HAND

1. Photocopy or trace the Link and Oval patterns (page 25).

2. Trace or transfer the design to a piece of card stock or template plastic.

3. Trace the template onto the kraft-tex using the fabric marker.

4. Cut out the links just inside the traced line.

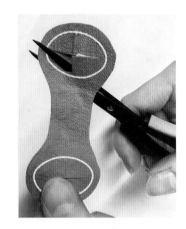

5. To cut out the inner ovals of the links, use the craft knife to cut a small slice in the center of each oval. Hold the link in your left hand and have the scissors come up through the hole. Trim inside the hole ¹⁄₁₆″ from the stitching.

6. Cut 30 Turquoise links, 1 Turquoise oval, and 25 Greenery links.

Preparing the Links

1. After cutting out the links, fold them in half at the center. Use the handle of your scissors to set the fold for a sharp crease.

2. To assemble the link rows, unfold 1 link. Insert it through the holes in 1 folded link and refold it. Continue until the row has 7 links. Assemble 4 Turquoise rows and 3 Greenery rows.

Finished bag: 13″ wide × 10″ high × 2″ deep

Construction

Use ½″ seams unless otherwise noted.

Prepare the Bag Pieces

1. Cut out all the pieces (see Cutting, page 6).

2. Fuse the interfacing to the corresponding fabric pieces according to manufacturer's instructions.

3. Photocopy or trace the Rounded Corner pattern (page 25) to make a template. Use it to trim the bottom corners of all front, back, and bottom flap band pieces. Do not trim the flap piece corners until after the links are in place.

4. At each lower corner of the front, back, and bottom pieces, make a mark 1½″ up and 1½″ over from the corner point with the fabric marker.

5. Align the arrows on the template with the marks on the fabric pieces and trace the curve with the fabric marker.

6. Trim the corner.

Make the Flap

1. Mark the placement of the link rows, using the fabric marker to draw a horizontal line across the flap piece 2⅜″ down from the top edge.

2. Measure in 1¾″ from the left cut edge and make a small dot on the line. Continue making 6 more dots across the line, spacing them 1¾″ apart.

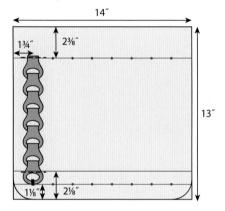

3. Draw another horizontal line 1⅛″ up from the bottom edge of the flap piece. Repeat Step 2 to mark dots across it in the same way you did for the upper line.

4. Draw one more horizontal line 2⅛″ up from the bottom edge of the flap piece. This will be the basting line for the bottom-most links.

5. Place the center of the folded edge of the top link of a Turquoise link row on the left-most dot and baste it to the flap piece close to the folded edge. Repeat with all the link rows, alternating the colors.

6. Align the bottom edge (loop edge) of the bottom-most link with the dot on the line at the bottom of the flap piece. Tack the link in place by hand or by machine. I used a wide zigzag stitch with zero length on my machine to do this.

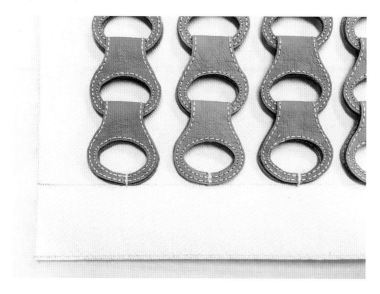

7. Baste across the bottom link just above the cutout oval for all rows (see the Step 2 drawing).

8. Use your Rounded Corner template to trim the bottom corners of the flap.

Cover the Link Row Ends

1. Press under ½″ on the top edge of the bottom flap band piece. Place the folded edge just above the marked line at the 2⅛″ line at the bottom of the flap. Edgestitch along the fold. Baste the remaining edges to the flap.

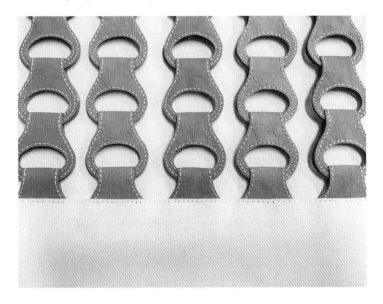

2. Press under ½″ on one long edge of the top flap band piece. Place the folded edge on the flap piece so it just covers the basting stitches that are holding the links in place. Edgestitch along the fold. Baste the remaining edges to the flap.

Attach the Lining to the Flap

With right sides together, stitch the flap lining piece to the flap, using a ½" seam. Clip the curved corners. Turn right side out and press. Topstitch around the flap ¼" from the edge, being careful not to stitch the links.

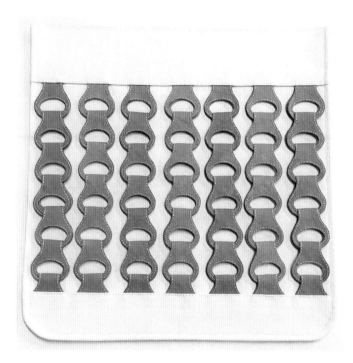

Make the Strap

NOTE

The strap is made with a top and bottom piece to avoid having to turn a thick, bulky tube.

1. Stitch the 2 strap top side pieces together at the short ends. Press open.

2. Repeat with the strap bottom side pieces.

3. Press under ½" to the wrong side along both long edges of the strap top side piece. Repeat with the strap bottom side piece.

4. With wrong sides together and the seams lined up, stitch the strap top to the strap bottom along both long edges, ⅛″ in from the edge. The strap top piece will extend beyond the bottom piece by ½″ at each end. This is to reduce bulk when the ends are folded and stitched.

5. Fold under the ½″ extended ends and press.

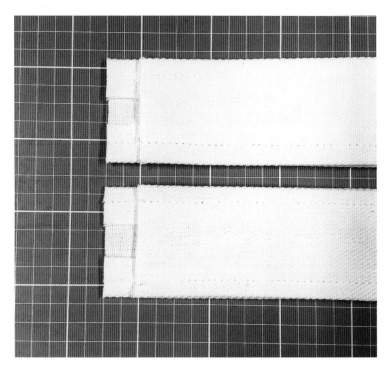

Make the Body of the Bag

1. Mark the center of the gusset piece on both long edges. Mark the center of the bottom edge of the front and back bag pieces.

2. Matching the centers, pin the gusset to the front. Stitch, clipping the gusset as necessary to go around the bottom curves. If you have a needle-down function on your machine, use it; and as you approach the curves, clip the gusset as you go.

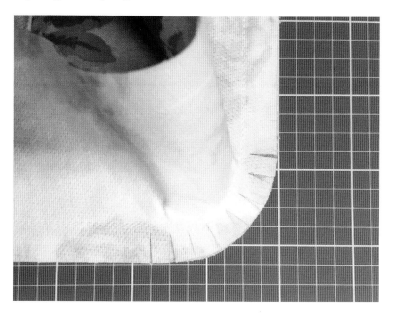

3. Repeat with the bag back.

4. Trim the ends of the gusset even with the bag fronts and back.

5. Press the seams open. Turn right side out and press.

Make the Hardware Tabs

1. Press under ½″ along the long edges of both pieces.

2. With wrong sides together, edgestitch the 2 pieces together just as you did for the strap.

3. Cut the piece in half horizontally to create 2 tabs.

Make the Lining

MAKE THE INNER POCKET

1. Clean finish the top edge of the pocket piece by pressing down ¼″ plus another ¼″, and edgestitch this hem in place.

2. Place the kraft-tex band centered and ¾″ down from the finished edge of the pocket. Edgestitch the band to the pocket. I used a decorative triple stitch to mimic the embroidered stitching on the links.

3. Press under ½″ along the side and bottom edges of the pocket.

4. Center the pocket on the back lining piece with the top edge of the pocket down 2″ from the top edge of the lining piece. Stitch the pocket to the lining.

COMPLETE THE LINING

1. Stitch the gusset to the lining front and back pieces in the same manner as the main fabric pieces.

2. Press the seams open, but leave the lining with the wrong sides out.

Put It All Together

1. Press each hardware tab in half horizontally. Insert each tab into 1 rectangle ring.

2. Baste the short edges of the tab together.

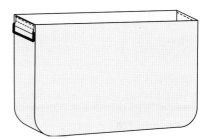

3. Pin 1 tab to the top edge of the gusset on the outside of the bag, centering it with raw edges even. Baste in place.

4. Repeat with other tab.

5. Baste the flap to the back of the outside of the bag with right sides together and raw edges even.

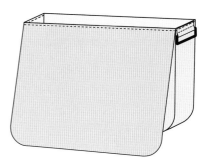

Attach the Lining

NOTE

The lining will be inserted and edge-stitched to the bag to avoid having to stitch and turn the bag.

1. Press under ½″ to the inside along the top edge of the bag, extending the flap and hardware tabs away from the bag. Press under ¾″ to the outside along the top edge of the lining. Having the lining a bit shorter than the bag helps prevent bunching of the lining.

2. Fit the lining into the body of the bag. Align the top folded edges and pin. Edgestitch along the top edge ⅛″ from the fold.

Attach the Strap

1. Insert one end of the strap into one side of the buckle, wrapping it around the center bar. Stitch the buckle in place along the folded end of the strap.

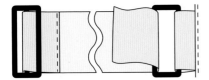

2. Pass the other end of the strap through the rectangle ring on one side of the bag and then thread it through the buckle.

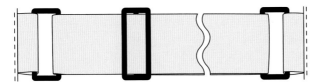

3. Pass that end through the other rectangle ring on the bag and turn it wrong side up.

4. Fold under the ½″ extension at the strap end, and fold the strap over the ring.

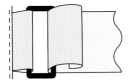

5. Stitch the fold close to the ring.

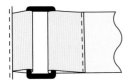

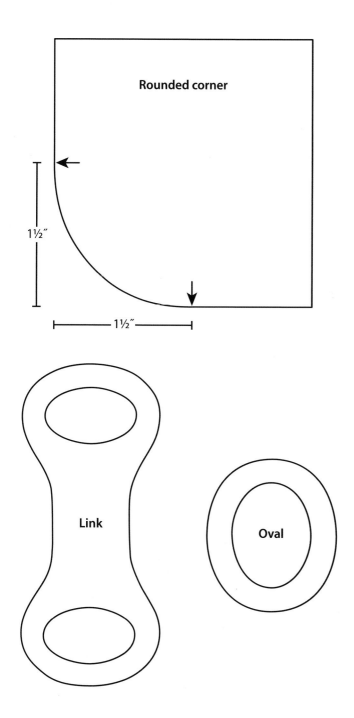

Rounded corner

1½"

1½"

Link

Oval

Finished wristlet: 7½˝ wide × 5˝ high

Construction

Use ½˝ seams are used unless otherwise noted.

Assemble the Front Panel

1. Cut out the links and center oval (see Creating the Links, page 10). Fold the links and assemble as shown in the photo.

2. Cut out all the pieces (see Cutting, page 6).

3. Fuse the interfacing to the corresponding fabric pieces.

4. Baste the contrast panel to the front main fabric piece.

5. Draw a vertical line ⅞˝ in from each side edge. Align the inner edge of the oval cutout of the outermost links with the marked lines. Have the top of the inner oval 2˝ down from the top edge of the front wristlet piece.

6. Baste the link assembly on the front piece as shown. Trim off the remainder of the links beyond the stitching.

7. Press under ¼″ along one long edge of each side band piece.

8. Edgestitch the side bands in place, having the side raw edges even.

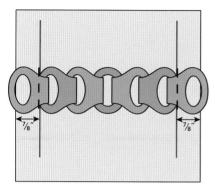 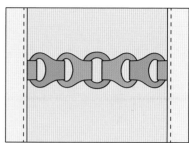

Make the Strap

1. Fold the long edges of the strap piece to the center and press.

2. Center the kraft-tex piece on the pressed strap, covering the raw edges.

3. Edgestitch the kraft-tex to the strap. I used a decorative triple stitch to mimic the embroidered stitching on the links.

4. Fold the strap in half and baste it to the left side of the front, 1¼″ down from the top, having raw edges even.

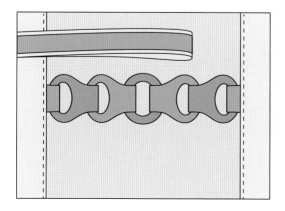

Prepare the Zipper

1. Press the 1¼" × 3" piece in half lengthwise.

2. Fold the long edges in again so they meet in the middle and press.

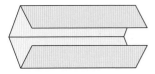

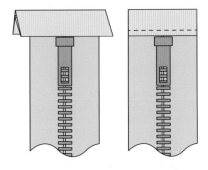

3. Cut the pressed piece into 2 pieces 1½" long.

4. Baste the zipper tape together just below the top zipper stop and trim the tape close to the stitching.

5. Encase that end of the zipper in one of the folded tab pieces and edgestitch in place.

6. Measure down along the zipper from the top of the encased end to 7¼" and mark it with the disappearing-ink fabric marker.

7. Zigzag over the zipper teeth at the mark, by hand or machine, and trim the excess zipper close to the stitches.

8. Encase that end in the other folded tab piece and topstitch in place.

9. Trim the tab pieces to the same width as the zipper. The zipper, including the encased ends, should measure 7¼".

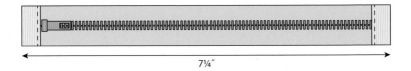

7¼"

Attach the Zipper

1. With right sides together, center the zipper along the top edge of the wristlet front, with the zipper stop toward the left edge. Stitch the zipper to the wristlet front, using a zipper foot.

2. Press the fabric away from the zipper.

3. Stitch the other side of the zipper to the back wristlet piece. Press.

4. Topstitch along both sides of the zipper.

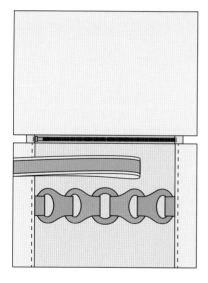

5. With right sides together, stitch the lining pieces to each wristlet piece along the top edge, sandwiching the zipper between the 2 layers. Press each lining piece away from the zipper.

6. Unzip the zipper halfway.

7. Pin the main fabric pieces right sides together, lining up the edges.

8. Pin the lining pieces right sides together, lining up the edges. Place the seam at the zipper fold toward the lining.

9. Stitch around the edges, using a ½″ seam.

10. Leave an opening at the bottom edge of the lining for turning.

11. Turn the wristlet right side out through the lining opening.

12. Press.

13. Slipstitch or topstitch the opening in the lining closed.

Finished key fob: 1¼˝ wide × 6½˝ long

1. Fold the long edges of the strap piece to the center, wrong sides together, and press.

2. Center the kraft-tex piece on the strap over the raw edges and edgestitch in place. I used a decorative triple stitch to mimic the embroidered links.

Photo by Kelly Burgoyne of C&T Publishing, Inc.

3. Fold the strap in half, aligning the cut ends.

4. Place the ends in the key fob hardware and crimp.

5. Thread the split ring key ring onto the crimped hardware piece.